Thoughts of a dog walker.

This is the page no one reads. It contains all the legal blah, blah we are obliged to tell you. I will warn you it contains a swearword - a really bad one. So now you probably will read it.

Published by Headless Chicken books. Part of nothing.
Address
www.headlesschickenbooks.com
First published in England 2014.

978-0-9926252-1-4

Also by this author:

'Poems by the Fourth most
famous bloke from Doncaster'
(2013).

Dedicated to Fred, Ruby, George and Elsie, without whom this book would be called 'The thoughts of The Loafer on the Sofa'. And probably not written.

21st Century hen-pecked man

My wife sends me a text
When she goes away
Of tasks to do
Several for each day

I always send her a text
Telling her what I've done
And of course, being me
I have a little fun

'Darling, I've mown the kitchen
Painted the strimmer
Put the recycling in the dry
    cleaners
Got Fairy Liquid for dinner

I've bought half a ton of
    butter
250 grams of fresh logs
Changed the stairs
Washed 3 loads of dogs

I've put (as requested)
Fresh sheets on the shed
Filled the car with milk
Put clean daffs in the bed

See, I can cope
When you're in a foreign land
See you soon
Your Loving Husband'

George Cooper

Yesterday morning our dog George
Traced his family tree
To his Great-great-great-great-
    great-great granddad
Way back in 2003

History repeating itself

On the Christmas Day truce
In the First World War
When we played the Germans at
    football
What was the score?

I have a horrid feeling
After the ref blew for full time
We lost in a penalty shoot out
In the mud and the grime

The 104th Most Famous Bloke from Doncaster

Suddenly everyone is
An expert on who's from
My hometown Doncaster
What is going on?

I think the title of Book One
Despite being self-deprecating
Has riled a lot of folk –
They find it irritating

A local I didn't know
Stopped me in the street
'So and so's more famous'
And that was in Crete

Diana Rigg, Charlie Williams
Lesley Garrett, Brian Blessed
Apparently the founder of DFS
Though on that better less said

'Paddington Bear's more famous'
Though as we're all aware
He's from Darkest Peru
And is actually a (fictitious) bear

One Direction's Louis Tomlinson
(pause for the girls to scream)
The guitartist from 'Babyshambles'
Continuing the musical theme

The founder of the Quakers
The bloke who started Methodism
God, my cockiness is waning
And being replaced by pessimism

Index-linking modes of transport

If penny farthings were built to-
    day
They'd have gone up several
    shillings
They'd be the '50p/20p coin bike'
Which would really rattle your
    fillings

Write shite

My writing used to be neat
I practiced and practiced
Now even doctors would
Say 'Blimey, what is this?'

I wrote a letter today (oh boy)
It looked as if an arthritic spider
Had written something
After a night out with Shaun Rider

Flower power

Rather than a sliding cost scale
I think florists should sell
Flowers by what you've done wrong
I know this would do well

The 'entry level' bunch
For 'I'm sorry I was late'
When you got home at midnight
When it should have been at half 8

Next rung up the ladder
'I forgot our anniversary'
Slightly dearer, natch
But worth it, you will see

A tastefully wrapped bunch
Of Peonies or wild roses
A snip to stop the danger
A woman with scissors poses

As the crimes increase
So does the cost
But they may well save your life
When your whole world looks lost

Next cab off the rank
And even dearer still
'I'm seeing another woman
She used to be called Bill'

Last on the menu of shame
Will cost you an arm and a leg
The 'In the last election, darling,
I voted for Nick Clegg'

<u>I've been bitten and will now write</u>
<u>a nasty poem to exact my revenge on</u>
<u>a certain insect. So there.</u>

A humming bird, no surpise
Makes a hum as it flies
The Blackbird is jet black
On its chest, wings and back

Mountaintops support mountain
    goats
Wire haired Vizsla, wiry coats
A Boa constrictor, so they say
Constricts the very last breath
    from its prey

The Crest ed Warbler (go, on,
    guess)
Has a lovely warble and a crest
So I scratch my head and wonder why
The mosquito isn't called the
    Bastard Fly

It's OK, they've already signed the
house over to me and my brothers

I wanted to talk to my Mother
But didn't feel very chatty
And came up with a brainwave
I think is rather natty

I call her at 7.25
(Oh this idea's so neat)
5 minutes before the start
Of Coronation Street

I heard the theme tune
'Nah nah nah nahnanah'
And in 2 seconds she said:
'I've got to go, tarrah'

Worth it?

Watch the girls in the ads on the
    telly
And before you hand over your money
Ask, 'What do they put in shampoos
That make your neck muscles go
    funny?'

Cultural desert

Going to the theatre?
I have tried that
Given a choice
I'd rather be Roy Keane's cat

Lads' Mag

I got the idea for a Lads' mag
It's based on what I'd like myself
It won't be really racy
So it won't be on the top shelf

It's photos of ladies
From Glasgow to Pontefract
Going about duties
In a manner 'matter of fact'

Jenny from Halifax
She's our first photo shoot
We see her arrive in a van
Wearing a tight boiler suit

The photos continue
We admire her flowing locks
But what we really love
Is she is carrying a tool box

Instead of pointing at stuff
And giving the job to a man
She pulls from her capacious box
WD40 in a can

In seconds flat
The hinges squeak no more
Then she does the same thing
To the sturdy looking front door

She is warming up
Her ample bosom heaves
As she wanders into the back yard
And rakes up all the leaves

In the front room
In this ever lengthening caper
She gets out a table
And starts to hang some wallpaper

A button pops on her boiler suit
You probably think 'Ding dong'
In a flash she pulls out a sewing
    kit
And sews the little critter back on

She turns her attention then
To the man watching tv
He seems happy as she hands over
A biscuit and a cup of tea

In the last page of pictures
She shakes him by the hand
Drives off in her Ford Transit
I hope this mag's not too bland

Dumped, for Nobody

I have always said
'No one is better than me'
I believe it, we all should
But an ex took it literally

She moved out of my flat
She left me for nobody
The oddest day of my life
Well, at least in the top 3

If she had said, 'Torquil, sorry
    Mark
As she rolled over in bed
I could have said she prefers
    another
And gone and kicked in his head

Not that I am a violent type
It would have helped a bit
Or a small clue like 'I want
    someone
Richer, cuter and with wit'

If she fancied an Asian bloke
A midget or basketball player
At least it would have made sense
If she ran off with the bassist
    from Slayer

She could have joined a convent
Or 'batted for the other side'
At least I can't compete
It wouldn't have battered my pride

Still it's not turned out too bad
I've got a pleasant enough life
Provided Jo hasn't eloped on her own
I'm just off to check on my wife

Shit.

I use the first shampoo I grab in
    the shower
'Colour Fix' it was called
I'm gutted as I'll be grey forever
Unless, of course, I go bald

End of the World

I'm glad the News of the World is
   no more
With its tales of scandal and sex
But the question is what do we now
   use
When we run out of Andrex?

Fry Day

What would Steven Fry do on a day
    off?
I bet he'd listen to Mötorhead
Wear a synthetic fibre shell suit
Read Jackie Collins in bed

I bet he'd play bingo online
Eat Pringles until he went pale
Watch Jeremy Kyle
Read the Daily Mail

He'd buy a two-litre bottle of cola
And do giant burps out loud
While singing the lyrics of Steps
To a non-existent crowd

He's constantly being brainy
Writing yet another article
'Did Keats actually find
The Higgs Boson particle?'

He must get exhausted
Being Steven Fry all the time
We should give him a day off
And here endeth this 'ere rhyme

Phwoah

I was driving yesterday
And the Land Rover began to smell
And I thought to myself
'F...' well, I'd better not tell

I sniffed to find out
What was causing the stink
Not the engine
I began to think

Is the wiring about to go
And catch fire?
On the A66
That would be dire

I opened the window and found
What'd made my brow sweat and
    furrow—
Was actually just the air
That hangs over Middlesbrough

I.

I often get asked
'Where do you get
The ideas for your poems?'
By folk I've just met

The same place
As everyone else, I say
I just shoehorn mine into a poem
Before I let them on their way

Pleb, a selfish one at that

People ask if you could go back
To any point in history
What year would you pick?
Where would you be?

My wife'd pick New York
In the roaring twenties
Pretty good
But not for me

How about Austria
In 1888 I think
The night Mr Hitler came home
Having gone to the pub for a
    drink?

Before he reached his wife
With whom he fancied his chances
I would knock him out
And stop passionate advances

No, if I could go back
I'd go back four days
When me and my sunglasses
Parted our ways

This sounds selfish
Possibly even trite
But I rarely find sunglasses to
    suit
Try as I might

But I have a large head
And my mother's small nose
Unless you do, you won't under-
    stand
The difficulty this does pose

I have finally managed to use the word 'phlegm' in a poem

I am in Hurley
The posh town not the actress
And compared to everyone else's
My Barbour's a right mess

It's covered in mud
Phlegm and god knows what
Down the fraying arms
There are trails of snot

On everyone else's Barbour
The only sign of dirt or wear
Is Range Rover seatbelt chaffing
Across the right shoulder

March 31st

At two minutes past midnight
I shook my wife awake
I whispered in her ear
'I just heard a window break'

'I think someone's broken in'
Her face went a shade of white
Not a shade Dulux make
It was a look of fright

'Ha ha, April Fool' I said
I can't repeat what she said
But I can report that
We have a comfortable spare bed

Hello, Goodbye

When people come to stay
We make them feel comfy
We drink fine wine
Jo cooks up some fine tea

Their bed sheets Egyptian 400 count
From the White Company
You'll have to ask my wife
It means FA to me

But what we do
Which is dead funny
Is send in the 8-legged alarm
    clock
Before we deliver morning tea

The dogs lick guests' feet
Have them screaming a lot
But it doesn't half work
They're up like a shot

We turn down the heating
After a couple of days
To actively encourage
The parting of our ways

We call it our MacDonald's
    approach
They make their seats of hard
    plastic
To get you to eat and go
Which seems a little drastic

Well, drastic if you get spotted
We're far more subtle, I'd say
Drop by some weekend
And please bugger off on Monday

'It could be you ...'

I have just had a shave
I have de-haired my nose
Brushed my teeth and hair
Put on my best clothes

I've checked my undies are clean
I put on some aftershave, nice
Well, it could be my turn today
To marry Katie Price

At last

It's the moment
You have been waiting for
It's poem number
twenty-four

Car talk

Gangsta-style Range Rover
The 'tinted rear window'
Why do they fit them?
Well, I think I know

It's not to hide what they're up to
So the world cannot see
It's to conceal the fact
Their kids are rather ugly

The Charlatans

Who has ever seen
The Phd or MA certificate
Of Messrs Hook and Dre?
We need to investigate

After we've busted all the fake
    Docs
Next will be the 'Professors'
Griff and Green beware
We're coming to settle scores

And they will laugh
Take a while to convince
But cast your mind back if you
    will
To 80's rockster 'Prince'

Yep, he was so scared that

He had to change his name
To something completely stupid
To avoid the inevitable shame

And Gaga will go gaga
Impersonating the artistocracy
She'll end up in The Tower
Just you wait and see

SPAM, SPAM, SPAM, SPAM ....

This morning
I sat down with a tea
Opened my inbox
To check who'd emailed me

Some guy called Mike Peng
Was offering translation
He offered it in the language
Of virtually every nation

8 American cents
He charges for each word
He translates for you
Which doesn't sound absurd

I sent him a reply
I can't type its contents
But for him to translate it
It would cost 16c

India from your sofa

If you haven't been to India
I have a little tip
To find out what it's like
Without the expense of a trip

Turn the colour, brightness and
    volume
As high as they'll go on your telly
And it will be exactly the same
As walking the streets of Dehli

Marriage

My missus is having a migraine
I have renamed it
A 'wegraine' as we all
Suffer her shit

Poet o'clock

I have a coffee at 6.30
And then a second cup
I have to get up this early
It's when my poet wakes up

Anti-War poem

If Tony Blair's surname was
   'Ducker'
It'd make life easier for me
Especially when writing
Some anti-war poetry

The truth. (Feat W. Wordsworth)

'I wandered lonely
As I haven't got any mates'
Was the original version
Of one of poetry's greats

More ammo for my wife's divorce lawyer

I told my wife tonight
She was looking hot
She smiled and said 'thanks'
And I said 'what?'

Our wires were crossed
I thought she was overheating
From cooking the meal
I was sitting eating

Credit card/telephone sale japery

'How does your name appear on the
    credit card?'
'Raised gold letters' I say
They either laugh or think 'dick-
    head'
And carry on any way

Pop in the kitchen

I just been in the kitchen
For my early morning fix
(Before you panic, ladies
It's just four Weetabix)

(Alpro Soya milk (light)
One spoon of brown sugar
If you insist on
Being a nosey bugger)

We have a new dishwasher
Fridge, washing machine and
    kettle
A whole kitchen of new 'White
    goods'
(Though they're all polished
    metal?)

They all have alarms and buzzers
To annoyingly remind you
You've left a door open
Or 'Cooee, I've defrosted your
    stew'

But this morning as I approached
They all went off simultaneously
It was like being at a Kraftwork
    gig
Circa 1983

I scream

Am I the only person
Told by his old man
That the ice cream man plays tunes
When he HAS ice creams in his van?

The Great Wall of China?

I've seen the Great Wall
The one in China, obviously
And the Wonders of the World
The 'must see' one, apparently

It took centuries to construct
It's visible from space
Thousands died as it was made
A Health and Safety disgrace

As I looked at it
I was going to say 'admiringly'
But I felt something
Gnawing away inside me

All its scale showed
If you're a bastard to lots of
    slaves
You can build massive things
Including walls (and mass graves)

Next week ... 'The Pyramids, shit
or what?'

Well I never ...

I was watching a documentary
About the Amazon
And every minute
A massive area is gone

An area the size of
Three football pitches disappears
Every single minute
It almost had me in tears

My sadness turned to surprise
I didn't suspect at all
That the Amazonians
Were that keen on football

<u>'Let it go man ...'.</u>
<u>'No'.</u>

I'm watching Grand Designs
They're restoring an old cottage
It's got a thatched roof
Which were once all the rage

Sadly I remember the '80s
And I'd rather get wet in the rain
Than employ a 'thatcher'
To rebuild the roof once again

A fisherman's tale

My wife says I don't
Buy flowers like I used to
Which I have to admit
Is probably true

But like I explained to her
Fishermen do not throw bait
At a fish already on the hook
Which she didn't think was great

Lordy

It is often said
In historic occasions
People can remember
Their precise locations

I can remember where I was
The Day The Music Died
Posh Spice's first single release
My, how I cried

Luckily my wife got to the radio
And turned it off
As I picked up some scissors
About to 'Do a Van Gogh'

Hoodies and how to get rid of them

In the '70s kids wouldn't be seen
    dead
Dressed like a Mod or a Ted
And why did they think it so sad?
T'was the teenage uniform of their
    Dad

'Get rid of hoodies', as some seem
    to insist
What do we do to make kids desist?
In two minutes flat they would be
    gone
If all their Dads just went and got
    one

Godliness

If 'cleanliness' is next to 'god-
    liness
It's pretty obvious to me
That some cheeky buggers
Ripped pages from your diction-
    ary

Memory test

What was the title of the last
    poem?
You have probably forgotten
Either it was instantly forget-
    table
Or your memory is rotten

My Mother-in-law's doctor
After my wife's request
Was asked similar questions
In her memory test

My test for her:
I ask her to lend me a pound
And if she tells me to bugger off
I know her mind's still sound

Brain power

We'd need fewer power stations on
    earth
If we were sold New York's elect-
    ricity at night
And we sold our electric
To countries that are to our right

Following on this thinking
The government of Khazakhstan
Could sell their nocturnal electric
That could help power Japan

Going further, Japan could sell
Their nighttime surplus, say
To the West of America
Portland or LA

The circle is complete
When New York is lit
By volts from California
Makes sense, doesn't it?

Change my name to increase sales?
Never, maybe, well OK

To boost sales I might call this
    book
'The Poems of Harry Porter'
Next to you-know-who on the shelf
It should sell, well it ought to

I suppose I could go another way
Change my name to J K Rowlett
I would sell by the millions
And bring my lawyers out in a sweat

Perhaps I could call it
Jordan: The Autobiography
Part 6 or 7 (what we up to now?)
Though she'd probably also sue me

Shakesbeer, Oscar Mild
Perhaps Bill Bry Nylon
A list that I fear
Could go on and on and on

It's not rocket surgery

I thought of this title
And not where it was going
So I am now stuck with
A good title and crap poem

White van man

I met Phillip earlier
Out with his Weimaraners
We had a chat about
Our usual mid life dramas

He told me of his van
He'd bought the night before
A battered old Vauxhall
From 1994

I said 'It's good to have
A decent size van
Very practical
For your modern man'

He was confused and asked
What I was on about
I said it's good for when
Your missus chucks you out

Well, he laughed and laughed
Till he was almost choking
And what's even funnier was
I wasn't even joking

A perfect couple

Do you reckon in a morning
Brad goes 'Christ it's Angelina
    Jolie'
When he wakes up and finds her in
    his bed
Or is that thought unique to me?

Do you reckon in a morning
Angelina goes 'Woo hoo, it's Brad
    Pitt'
When she finds him in her bed
Or is this also just daft shit?

Tee hee hee

My wife's cousin's husband
Yesterday took her away
For a romantic weekend
'Ahhhhhh' the girls all say

All the men from the north
All the way to the south
Will snigger when they hear
He's taken her to Cockermouth

Every poetry book has at least one
serious poem. This is that poem.

Are you a no-mark fool
Desperate to look cool
American, spotty and of teenage
Why not go on a shooting rampage?

Everyone in the world
Will know you as it unfurled
After 30 minutes of shame
6 billion will know your name

But I have a simple idea
So simple it might seem insincere
But why are the kids rampaging
What is it that they are a craving?

We could have a massive debate
About missing fathers or being
    overweight
But I think from the way they be-
    have
It is simply recognition they crave

So why not cut off the 'fame'
That the media will gift their name
Give them and their faces NO pub-
    licity
And hey presto they'll be no shoot-
    ing spree

<u>To celebrate the up and coming 40th</u>
<u>anniversary of the getting together</u>
<u>of The Edge, Bono, Larry and the</u>
<u>other one, I have written the</u>
<u>following song:</u>

Happy birthday U2
Happy birthday U2 ...
Etc. etc

A poem about Long Haired Dave (The poem Long Haired Dave has been dreading)

When I first started working
I had two mates called Dave
Who'd come to the agency bar
To chase skirt and misbehave

The charming WCRS receptionists
Would call up to my office
'Dave's here for you
Presumably to go on the piss'

I'd say 'which one?'
She'd say 'Long Haired Dave'
Long hair was quite novel
Post hippy, pre-rave

His hair is now about as long
As this book is thick
It's receded ever so slightly
But the nickname did stick

'Long Haired Dave'
With every hair that comes out
It gets 0.01% funnier
Without a shadow of a doubt

The P-Plan Diet

I saw John Cooper-Clark
On the telly last night
Boy is he skinny
It gave me a fright

If he is the most successful
Poet of his generation
I might need to consider
My employment situation

If that is how little food
A top poet can afford
I'll jump out of the poetry plane
And pull my ripcord

Useless xmas presents

'A wine stopper for if you only
    finish
Half of your bottle' they say
I laughed and laughed so much
I nearly spilled my pint of Char-
    donnay

Bob Hope

I just watched an item
On the ten o'clock news
And as you might expect
I have some half-arsed views

Cannabis 'farmers' can grow
A million pounds worth
In a semi-detached house in a
    year
Surely the best farmers on earth

Why not put them in charge
Of growing barley and wheat?
They'll easily grow enough
For the whole world to eat

Imagine what they could grow
Given a whole field
Based on what you can get
A 2 up 2 down to yield

Country 'living' in Richmond

At 8.30 pm the only activity
Is the bloke in his van
Unloading the tumbleweed
And turning on his giant fan

<u>F*** M*</u>

You can tell how it's doing
Your loving relationship
By how quickly the radio's put on
When you're out in the car on a
    trip

For years we always spoke
Both eager to know
'How was your day?'
Never touched the radio

After about 5 years
The radio would go on
Just about junction nine
On the A1

As the years crawled by
Long before junction 2 was passed
We'd be silently listening to
The Archers or shipping forecast

Now we don't even bother
The radio's always going
One day the talking just stopped
Without either of us noticing

Big hair

I fitted a new roof lining
In my Land Rover Defender
I know you don't care
But it's my poem remember

I use the roof lining
As a device to tell me
When I need a haircut
My 'Morrissey, circa 1983'

The new roof is 2 inches higher
I've got a look you wouldn't dig
My quiff is 2 inches taller
I look like Elvis in an Elvis wig

The Late Mark Cooper

'Can I speak to Mark Cooper?'
"I am afraid he is dead"
I told the pesky telesales bloke
It went straight over his head

'When would be a convenient time
For me to call back?'
I could not believe his second
Angle of attack

'In his second life, after 9.45'
I should have said
But didn't think of it in time
And repeated 'He is dead'

'He is dead
Do you understand?'
There was a moment's silence
In some distant land

The rupee finally dropped
He apologised profusely
And within 2 milliseconds
He'd put down the phone on me.

'X'

I watch the X factor
Of a Saturday night
I can't get near the remote
There's always a bloody fight

I've spotted something though
The winners come from places
Where the call centres are
Which might put a smile on some
    faces

A poem to irritate my wife

My wife Jo doesn't like it
When I write a short poem
She's only gone and inspired one
Without her even knowing

Amerika

To our friends across the Atlantic
I would like to send my views
About the language
We kindly let you use

Colour has a 'u'
As does'favour'
And before you ask
I'm not a spelling bore

If you want to bastardise
(Note 's' not 'z')
Invent your own language
And wreck that instead

Top Trumps conversation

I met a geezer
In the pub last night
I'd tell you his name
But I forgot it, alright

He was obviously
A Top Trumps fanatic
When he was younger
And now he's a prick

Every thing I'd done
Every place I'd been to
He'd been there before and
More times than me and you

He'd been on more planes
Had more cars
Done more business
Met more stars

He knew a lot more about this
Way more about that
After just 10 minutes
I thought 'what a twat'

Mrs. Thatcher's River Cleaning Policy

We all slagged her off
Well, I did for sure
But she had her eyes
On the bigger picture

The River Don in Doncaster
Was so full of shit
You didn't need to be Jesus
To walk across it

Pallets and gas cylinders
Glowing blue toxic sediment
If it'd been any fuller of shit
It could've stood for parliament

But thanks to her broader view
The dirty factories are now gone
In Donny and Sheffield
Which has really helped The Don

See there's now no pollution
Pumped into the river
Everyone who criticised Thatcher
Should man up and forgive her

It now has lots of plant life
Even trout and salmon
That folk have time to admire
As they walk into town to sign on

25 carat desperation

If you thought this was funny
Please go and buy
My first book
You'll laugh till you cry

It'll also mean family members
Won't get the same present
Every Birthday/Christmas/anniv-
    ersary
Which they're starting to resent*

*'Poems by the fourth most famous
  bloke from Doncaster'is available
  from www.headlesschickenbooks.co.uk

Every cloud has an orange
   lining

When I was a kid
We got Airfix kits
But there was always one thing
That really got on my nerves

You'd build a Spitfire
It'd take the patience of a saint
Then as you set about painting it
You'd run out of the right paint

Now my views may appear picky
Or even a little old
But the Germans wouldn't have been
   scared
Of a Spitfire that was half gold

Many a Chieftain tank
That left my bedroom
Was two-thirds olive-green
One-third maroon

My HMS Ark Royal
Frankly, it was a sham
The upper decks gunmetal grey
The hull the colour of ham

Sadly Airfix are no more
Sunk by their paint supplier
Still, they've helped me a poem
    nearer
The day when I can retire